teddy bears

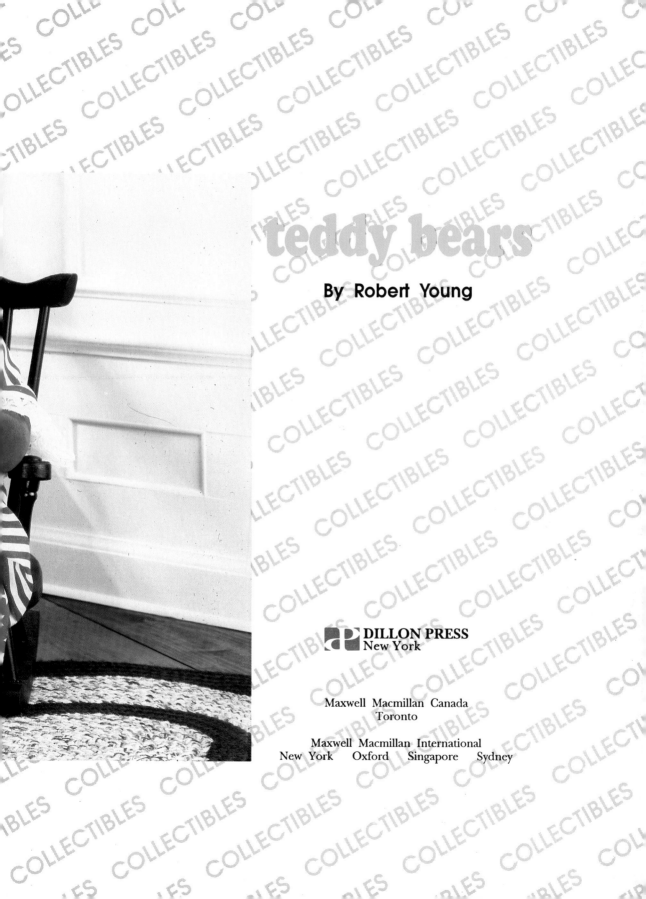

teddy bears

By Robert Young

DILLON PRESS
New York

Maxwell Macmillan Canada
Toronto

Maxwell Macmillan International
New York   Oxford   Singapore   Sydney

For Lavonne and Linda, who both love bears and books

Acknowledgments

Many thanks to the following people for their help on this book: Mary Fran Baldo, Bill Boyd, Betty Chan, Elsie Carper, Diane Cardinale, Wallace Finley Dailey, Barbara Dawson, Barbara Dike, David Goldberg, Delores Haddad, Pam Hommeyer, Linda Huston, Patty Johnson, The Keegans, Janice Kelly, Lavonne Klohn, Susan Leeson, Lisa Lloyd, Cheryl Maciorkoski, Terry Michaud, Linda Mullins, Margo Plummer, Patty Reese, Jim Samere, Rebecca Smith, Cathie Sotir, Joyce Stanton, Terrie Stong, Jim Swearingen, Rosemary Volpp, Elizabeth Wardley, Elizabeth Whelpley, Martha White, Barbara Wolters, Peggy Young, Sara Young, and Tyler Young.

Photo Credits

Front cover images by Smithsonian, Enesco, and North American Bear Company
Back cover image by Robert Young
Interior artwork: Bill Boyd, 32; Dakin, 38, 40, 42, 43, 44, 45; Dutton Children's Books, a division of Penguin Books USA, 31; Franny's Bear Museum, 16; Kenner Procucts, 35; Library of Congress, 26, 29; Lisa Lloyd, 8; Thomas J. Mocny, 9; Linda Mullins, 48, 51; North American Bear Company, title page, 6, 13; Theodore Roosevelt Collection, Harvard College Library, 18; Rosemary Volpp, 11; *Washington Post*, 20; Robert Young, frontispiece, 54.

Book design by Carol Matsuyama

Library of Congress Cataloging-in-Publication Data

Young, Robert (Scott), 1951-
  Teddy bears / Robert Young. — 1st ed.
    p.   cm. — (Collectibles)
  Includes index.
  Summary: Discusses teddy bears, their history, how they are made, the reasons for their popularity, and how to collect them.
  ISBN 0-87518-520-7
  1. Teddy bears—Juvenile literature. (1. Teddy bears.) I. Title. II. Series: Collectibles.
NK8740. Y68   1992
688.7´24—dc20   92-4347

Dillon Press   Maxwell Macmillan Canada, Inc.
Macmillan Publishing Company   1200 Eglinton Avenue East
866 Third Avenue   Suite 200
New York, NY 10022   Don Mills, Ontario M3C 3N1

Macmillan Publishing Company is part of the Maxwell Communication Group of Companies.

First edition

Printed in the United States of America

10   9   8   7   6   5   4   3   2   1

Abearham Lincoln, one of the many different kinds of bears people can choose from today

CHAPTER 1

Teddy!

What's to love about Teddy Bears? Everything. They are cute and cuddly. They are friendly and smile at everyone they see. You can take Teddy Bears anywhere you want to go. They won't complain or criticize you, either. They will comfort you when you're scared. They will listen to whatever you tell them, and they won't tell a soul.

People of all ages love Teddy Bears. Kids love to cuddle them, take them places, and play with them. Adults love them, too. Teddy Bears give them a chance to have fun and be silly. They remind adults of the days when they were kids. Having bears helps adults keep a part of their childhood forever.

Teddy Bears are only one of the many types of stuffed toys. These toys are called **plush*** by people in the toy industry. Plush is the soft, furlike fabric used as a covering on most of these toys.

Millions of Teddy Bears are made every year. They come in almost every shape, size, and color you can think of. There are bears small enough to fit into your pocket, and a bear so large it must be

*Words in **bold** type are explained in the glossary at the end of this book.

From tiny bears the size of your finger to giants (opposite page) as big as your house, bears come in all sizes.

carried in a 34–foot trailer. There are fuzzy bears and shorthaired bears. There are bears with noses to push and bears with hearts that beat. There are bears that growl, talk, and move. There are bears from books, historical bears, and bears that care about our world.

If you own Teddy Bears, you might want things that go with them. And so there are bear clothes of every imaginable style. There are costumes and jewelry for Teddy Bears to wear, and toys for Teddy Bears to play with.

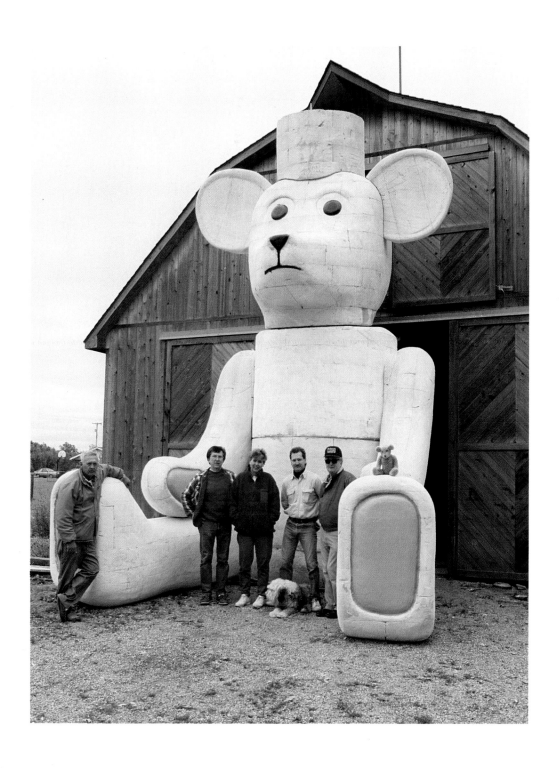

TEDDY BEARS

Teddy Bears have become a part of modern life. Thousands of people around the world collect them. There are Teddy Bear fairs, shows, and conventions. There are books and magazines on the subject of Teddy Bears. There are stores that sell only Teddy Bears, and there is even a Teddy Bear museum.

Older Teddy Bears are becoming more valuable because so many people want to collect them. The most expensive bear—one made by the Margarete Steiff Company in 1926—was bought in 1989 for more than $80,000 at a Sotheby's auction in London.

It was bought by Rosemary and Paul Volpp of Buena Park, California. They had wanted a special gift to celebrate their 42d wedding anniversary. They thought the Steiff bear would be the perfect gift and a nice addition to their Teddy Bear collection. The Volpps had a representative in London bid on the bear. But the bidding went far beyond the $10,000 they expected. It took a bid of $86,350 to make the bear theirs. Later they heard why the bidding had gone so high: They had been bidding against the royal family of England!

Don't think that Teddy Bears are only fun toys to play with and collect. Teddy Bears have also become a helpful part of our lives today.

Rosemary Volpp and Happy Anniversary, the valuable bear made in 1926 by the Steiff Company.

TEDDY BEARS

In schools, teachers use Teddy Bears to help get kids excited about learning. In kindergarten and first grade, for example, the bears are used to help children learn the alphabet and begin to read. They are a good learning tool because kids love them. Counselors use bears when kids need a special friend to help comfort them.

Hospitals use Teddy Bears in several ways. Some have "Bear Clinics" to which kids can bring their bears to have them repaired. This helps children learn about hospitals and feel more comfortable in them. Hospitals also use bears to comfort kids who are hurt, sick, or scared. Some even have bears that young patients can draw on and color.

Police and fire departments know how helpful Teddy Bears can be. Many get bears from charity organizations such as the Telephone Pioneers, Eastern Star, and the Assistance League. The bears, sometimes known as "bear buddies," are carried in police cars, ambulances, and fire trucks. They are given to children who have been hurt or have been victims of a crime.

With the help of organizations like Good Bears of the World (GBW), Teddy Bears have become a symbol for caring. GBW was started in 1969 by

Bears are often used in hospitals to comfort kids as well as teach them.

James T. Ownby after he read about a man who gave bears to children in hospitals. Since then, GBW has raised money, bought bears, and given them to both children and adults who need a special friend.

The Volpps use their famous bear, which they named Happy Anniversary, to help children. The Volpps take their bear to shows and conventions in the United States and England. People pay to see the bear, and the Volpps donate that money to

TEDDY BEARS

children's hospitals. In less than two years, Happy Anniversary raised more than $20,000.

Teddy Bears are now the most popular plush, with millions being made and sold each year. But that's only the beginning. Today, Teddy Bears are more than stuffed toys. There are hundreds of different Teddy Bear products, from neckties to notepads, from banks to bandages, from stickers to snacks. You can buy Teddy Bear jewelry, Teddy Bear Christmas ornaments, Teddy Bear telephones, and even a Teddy Bear car burglar alarm. Teddy Bears are so popular that they are used by some companies to help advertise their products.

How did this all happen? How did Teddy Bears become one of the most lovable and loved toys in history? It all started around the turn of the century.

- An **arctophilist** is a person who collects Teddy Bears.

- Frannie's Teddy Bear Museum in Naples, Florida, has more than 2,000 bears on display.

- Good Bears of the World named 1985 the Year of the Bear.

- The world's largest bear (see page 9) was made in 1989 by Keystone Traders Ltd. of Chesaning, Michigan. The bear, named Yankee Doodle Teddy, stands over 30 feet tall and weighs 1,930 pounds. The bear took 1,200 worker-hours to finish.

CHAPTER 2

Teddy Bear Beginnings

Teddy Bears may have become the most popular bears in history, but they weren't the first toy bears made. Toy bears were popular in many parts of the world during the 1800s. Russian bears, called Miskas, were traditional folk toys. In England, mechanical bears were made that moved, growled, and were covered with real fur. They were called Bruins.

The soft, cuddly bears we know today as Teddy Bears were not made until 1902. As to where the first Teddy Bears were made, that's another matter. Some people believe the first Teddy Bears were made in the United States because of a famous hunting trip by President Theodore (Teddy) Roosevelt.

In November 1902 Roosevelt traveled to the state of Mississippi. He went there because of a dis-agreement the people of Mississippi were having with their neighbors in Louisiana. They could not agree on where the states' boundary line should be. Roosevelt went to help them settle the dispute. But there was time for more than politics during the president's visit. He got a chance to go hunting,

An older bear—all dressed up for a party

Theodore Roosevelt—the "father" of all Teddy Bears—on a hunting trip

one of his favorite pastimes.

After several days of hunting for bears, the president was getting frustrated at not having gotten one. According to legend, to please the president, some men in his hunting party found a bear cub and tied it to a tree for him to shoot.

When Roosevelt saw the small bear, he was disgusted and angry. He ordered the men to let the bear go, saying, "I draw the line. If I shot that little fellow, I couldn't look my own boys in the face again."

A newspaper article reported the story differently. On November 16, 1902, the story was printed on the front page of the *Washington Post*. According to that story, a few men in Roosevelt's hunting party trailed a lean, black bear to a watering hole. There, although tired, the bear killed one of the hunting dogs before being hit over the head and tied up by the men.

When Roosevelt was called to the scene and saw the bear, he would not allow it to be shot. He didn't consider it "sporting" to shoot a tired, captive bear. Instead, he is reported to have said to the men, "Put it out of its misery." One of the hunters then quickly killed the bear with a hunting knife.

The next day a political cartoon by Clifford

Clifford Berryman's Washington Post *cartoon*

Berryman was printed in the *Washington Post*. The cartoon, titled "Drawing the Line in Mississippi," refers to the border dispute and shows Roosevelt refusing to shoot a full-grown bear. But this wasn't the only cartoon Berryman drew of the hunting incident. He drew another one showing a smaller, frightened bear. The bear in this cartoon may have helped start the story that the bear was only a cub.

While we can't be sure what kind of bear it was that Roosevelt refused to shoot, we can be sure that the incident got people thinking about bears. In Brooklyn, New York, a shopkeeper and his wife saw Berryman's cartoon and had an idea. They decided to make stuffed bears like the one the president wouldn't shoot.

Morris and Rose Michtom made these bears by hand and then displayed the first two in the window of their novelty and candy store. Seeing the bears displayed gave Morris another idea. He wrote to the president and asked permission to call the toys "Teddy's Bears," a name that was later shortened to "Teddy Bears." President Roosevelt wrote that he didn't know how his name could be of help, but that it was okay for Michtom to use it.

The Michtoms' bears were a quick success. So many people ordered them that the couple soon closed their store in order to work on the bears full-time. In 1903 they started their own toy company:

the Ideal Novelty and Toy Company.

Not everyone agrees that the Michtoms' bears were the first Teddy Bears. Some people think the first Teddy Bears were made in Germany.

Margarete Steiff was born in Giengen, Germany, in 1847. As a child she had polio, which paralyzed her legs and left her right arm weak. Margarete had a strong desire to be independent and earn her own living, in spite of her handicaps. She did this by sewing, even though she had to run the sewing machine backward. That way she could turn it with her left hand.

In 1877, Margarete opened her own ladies' and children's clothing shop. An imaginative seamstress, she began to sew pincushions in the shapes of elephants. These were so well liked with the neighborhood children that she decided to make larger elephant toys. The success of the elephants led her to make other stuffed toys: pigs, monkeys, horses, and camels. Margarete's brother Fritz sold her animals at local fairs.

By the end of the 1880s, Margarete Steiff's business had grown so much that her toys were being made in a factory. Even though there were many people working on the toys, Margarete still kept a close eye on production. She personally inspected each animal before it left the factory.

It took a few more years before stuffed bears became a part of the Steiff line of toys. Bears were added because of an idea by Richard Steiff, Margarete's nephew. Richard was an art-school graduate who enjoyed drawing animals. In 1897, Richard attended an animal show and sketched a family of brown bears. From these drawings, he designed a stuffed bear toy.

In 1903, Richard took the first Steiff bears to the Leipzig Trade Fair, where new products were shown. Not many people noticed the bears, but one important person did. That person was an American toy buyer who worked for the George Borgfeldt Company. He thought the bears would sell well in the United States, so he ordered 3,000.

In 1903 both the Michtom bears and Steiff bears sold well in the United States. And that was just the beginning of the "bear craze." By 1908, more than a million Teddy Bears were being sold each year.

It would be difficult, if not impossible, to credit one person for bringing us the first Teddy Bear. But we can credit several people for helping: President Theodore Roosevelt for hunting bears in Mississippi,

TEDDY BEARS

Clifford Berryman for creating the famous "hunting" cartoon, Morris and Rose Michtom for making their first bear, Richard Steiff for designing the first Steiff bear, and Margarete Steiff for producing it. All of these people helped give birth to one of the most popular toys in history.

- The Teddy Bear was invented as a toy for boys.

- The anniversary of Teddy Roosevelt's birth is October 27. Bear lovers around the world celebrate that day as "Good Bear Day."

- Clifford Berryman, who created the famous hunting" cartoon, worked for 63 years as a cartoonist and made 15,000 political cartoons.

- The first stuffed bear made by Morris and Rose Michtom had black shoe buttons for eyes.

- In 1903, Steiff made 12,000 stuffed bears. By 1907, the company was making nearly one million bears a year. To prevent other companies from copying its bears, Steiff attached a small metal button to one of each bear's ears. This button became the company's trademark.

- Steiff Teddy Bears were used as table decorations at the wedding of President Teddy Roosevelt's daughter, Alice, in 1906.

- The Ideal Novelty and Toy Company, started by Morris and Rose Michtom, became one of the largest toy manufacturers in the United States.

By 1908 more than a million Teddy Bears were being sold each year in the United States. Bear factories like this one sprang up all over the country.

CHAPTER 3

Teddy Bears through the Years

In 1903, Teddy Bears were being made by only two companies: the Margarete Steiff Company in Germany and the Ideal Novelty and Toy Company in the United States. But that changed quickly as Teddy Bears became popular. Within a few years many more companies in Germany started making Teddy Bears. In the United States, Teddy Bear factories were opening in almost every major city.

As Teddy Bears grew in popularity, people began to make clothes just for them. In 1906, two companies—Kahn and Mossbacher and D. W. Shoyer—started selling clothes such as sailor and clown outfits, overalls, and pajamas. Even underwear!

Other products were made for Teddy Bears, too. Wagons and circus carts were made. So were cages and pedal cars.

New kinds of Teddy Bears were made. There were musical bears, whistling bears, and laughing bears. There were bear dolls, two-faced bears, and tumbling bears. There was even a bear with eyes that lit up when you shook its right paw.

Teddy Bears became so popular that many other Teddy Bear products were made. Bear paper dolls, pins, baby rattles, postcards, and books were all being sold by 1910. Between the years of 1907 and 1911, more than 40 songs were written with Teddy Bears in their titles.

The United States and Germany weren't the only countries where Teddy Bears were popular. Many people in England loved bears, too. By 1909, English toy makers were starting to turn out Teddy Bears. They already had the parts to make bears, and they were lucky to be in a country with many Angora goats. The long, white, silky hair from these goats is called **mohair**, and it makes a great covering for stuffed toys.

The Teddy Bears made in England were a lot like the bears made by Steiff and Ideal. They were jointed at the head and body, stuffed with curled wood shavings, and had devices in them that made them growl when they were tipped.

Still, there were differences. The English bears were plumper than the bears made in Germany and the United States. They also had shorter arms,

As the "bear craze" swept the nation, kids thought of all different ways to play with their new toys.

shorter noses, and wider heads.

By 1920, changes had already begun in the making of Teddy Bears. New materials, such as **kapok**, a natural fiber, were being used to stuff some bears. Glass, in addition to buttons, was being used to make eyes, and leather was used on the paw pads. Growlers that worked when they were squeezed were used as well as tilt growlers.

The year 1920 was an important one in Teddy Bear history. That was when Daphne Milne bought a Teddy Bear, at Harrods in London, for her son's first birthday. Daphne's husband, A. A. Milne, was a magazine writer. Their son, Christopher Robin Milne, loved the bear and named it Winnie-the-Pooh. The name Winnie came from a bear Christopher Robin liked at the zoo; the name Pooh came from a swan he enjoyed feeding.

Christopher Robin's adventures with his favorite bear gave his father the idea of writing stories about them. These stories brought Winnie-the-Pooh to life and made him known throughout the world. The first Winnie-the-Pooh story was published in 1926. The well-loved tales quickly led to the making of Winnie-the-Pooh stuffed toys.

Winnie-the-Pooh is not the only bear to have come from a book. Rupert Bear and Paddington Bear, both from England, have been popular over the years. So has SuperTed, a bear with magical powers. And, of course, there are the Berenstain Bears.

Not all Teddy Bears in history have been so loved. Between 1925 and 1928, the Gebrüder

Winnie-the-Pooh with A. A. Milne and Cristopher Robin

Sussenguth Company in Neustadt, Germany, made a bear they called Peter. It had a realistic face with glass eyes that rolled from side to side and a mouth that opened to show large, sharp teeth. Its growler was loud and fierce-sounding.

Peter was not the cute, cuddly bear that people were used to. In fact, it scared so many children that the company stopped selling it, so there are very few around today. Peter is thought

Peter, the bear nobody liked

by many to be the rarest Teddy Bear in history. It is valued at between $2,500 and $4,000.

In spite of bears like Peter, interest in Teddy Bears continued to grow. More Teddy Bear companies were started and more varieties of bears were made. In the late 1940s, the first battery-operated bears were produced. There were many different kinds of moving bears: artist bears, blacksmith bears, dentist bears, clown bears, and bears that played musical instruments. Most battery-operated bears were made in Japan because of the low labor costs there at that time.

Along with popularity came concerns about safety—not only of Teddy Bears but toys in general. As early as the 1930s, toy makers began working with groups like the National Safety Council to make sure toys would not be harmful to children. Organizations were formed in 1946 and 1958 so that people could report injuries, and in 1969 laws were passed to make sure toys were safe. In 1973 more laws were passed and the United States Consumer Product Safety Commission (CPSC) was formed. The CPSC makes and enforces safety rules for toys and other children's products.

The new laws brought about changes in Teddy Bears. New stuffings—cleaner and more fire resistant—were used. Button or glass eyes were replaced with plastic eyes. Improvements were made so that the small parts of bears would not come off and be swallowed by young children. New methods and materials helped to make seams stronger and less likely to break.

The CPSC is still working today. It investigates complaints about toys, including Teddy Bears. If officials find that a product is not safe, they make sure it is not sold.

During the 1970s, more and more people began collecting Teddy Bears as a hobby. For some collectors, the love of Teddy Bears became the start of a new career. They began designing, making, and selling their own bears. By the mid-1980s, there was a great demand for handcrafted Teddy Bears.

But Teddy Bear artists weren't the only ones making creative bears. Barbara Isenberg, a New York writer, enjoyed making toys for her son. Her first Teddy Bear was made out of sweatshirt material. That bear became Albert the Running Bear, which led to more interesting designs. Before long, Isenberg started the North American Bear Company and was selling bears such as William Shakesbear, Bearsy Ross, and the Statue of Libearty.

In 1983, Kenner Products came out with Care Bears. These bears were made to help children express their feelings of love, friendship, and caring. Each Care Bear character came in a different color with a special design on its stomach and a story attached. Each had its own personality. More than 20 million Care Bears were sold in five years.

A year later, Carolyn and Lawrence Shaffer, heart surgeons and Teddy Bear collectors, created

A pair of Care Bears. These friendly characters were introduced in 1983 and became an instant success.

Sir Koff-A-Lot. Sir Koff-A-Lot is a firmly stuffed 17-inch bear used for adults who've had surgery. Patients hold the bear against their chests to reduce pain when they have to cough. Some 25,000 Sir Koff-A-Lots are sold each year in 44 different states.

And, of course, there's Teddy Ruxpin, the high-tech bear that came on the market in 1985. This bear took the mechanical bears of the 1800s and the battery-operated bears of the 1940s one giant step forward. With the help of a computer, tiny motors, and a cassette player hidden inside him, Teddy

Ruxpin talked as well as moved. Did the public like Teddy Ruxpin? More than a million were sold the first year!

Teddy Bear lovers are very lucky because there are millions of bears made each year. There are many different kinds, too. One company, Dakin, makes 50 varieties of Teddy Bears. Other large companies like Gund, Applause, and Steiff also make many kinds of bears. So do hundreds of Teddy Bear artists. Today, you can find a Teddy Bear in any shape, size, and price range. You can find Teddy Bears made of almost any kind of material, from plastic to wood to glass.

What is to become of Teddy Bears? What does the future hold? The future of Teddy Bears looks as bright as its past. Who could possibly picture a world without our favorite stuffed toy? What would you cuddle? Who would you tell your secrets to? Because of the way they make us feel, Teddy Bears will always have a place in our hearts. The only limit on the varieties and uses of Teddy Bears will be our imagination.

- By A. A. Milne's death in 1956, his Winnie-the-Pooh stories had been translated into 25 languages and had sold more than seven million copies. The original Pooh bear now lives at the children's room of the Donnell branch of the New York Public Library.

- 97 percent of children in America recognize the name Care Bears.

- The 1991 version of the Care Bears was a bear that cared about the environment.

- Dakin is the largest maker of stuffed toys in the United States. The company began in 1955 as an importer of shotguns and toy trains.

- Sir Koff-A-Lot bears are used in more than 200 hospitals throughout the United States.

- Teddy Ruxpin was the most popular toy in the United States in 1985.

The first step in making a Teddy Bear: drawing the design on paper.

CHAPTER 4
Making Teddy Bears

Millions of Teddy Bears are made every year. Some bears are handmade by hobbyists or Teddy Bear artists. Most bears, though, are made in factories by toy companies.

Making bears in factories takes special machines and people with special skills. But before a bear can be made, it must be designed. A designer begins with an idea and then makes a drawing. From the drawing a **prototype**, or full-size model, is made by hand.

The prototype is carefully considered. The designer checks to see if the prototype matches the original idea. The quality-control department reviews it to make sure it is safe. People in the sales department estimate the price of the bear and how many could be sold at that price. People in the production department figure out what it would cost to make the bear. Working together, these last two departments determine how much profit the company would make by producing the bear. If it's enough, the company decides to go ahead and make and sell the bear.

Dies, positioned on layers of plush, will be used to cut out the shapes of the bear.

Once a bear prototype has been chosen, several things must be done. Rolls of plush, yards of fabrics, boxes of stuffing, and parts for the bears must be ordered from the companies that make them. **Dies**—sharp metal devices used to cut out the pieces of plush—must be made. When all the parts and materials have been gathered at the factory, production can begin.

In the first stage of production, the plush is cut

into pieces that will make up the bear. Several layers of plush are unrolled onto a long table. About 20 dies of different shapes and sizes are placed onto the plush. The plush and dies are then put into a machine. The machine presses down hard on the dies with thousands of pounds of pressure, making them cut through the plush.

The cut pieces of plush are taken to the sewing room, where workers sew the pieces together by machine, one by one. The pieces are sewn inside out so that the stitching will not be seen. A small opening is left on the back of the bear so that the stuffing can be blown in later.

At this point, the bear is looking more like an empty bag than a stuffed toy. It has a shape, but no insides or even a face. But that soon changes. With the help of a special machine, the eyes are put on.

The back of each eye is connected to a plastic bolt. The bolt is pushed through the plush of the bear's face and a washer is put on the end. The eye is then put into a machine that pushes the washer along the bolt until it's snug. This keeps the eye tight, making it very difficult to be pulled off. Young children have been known to

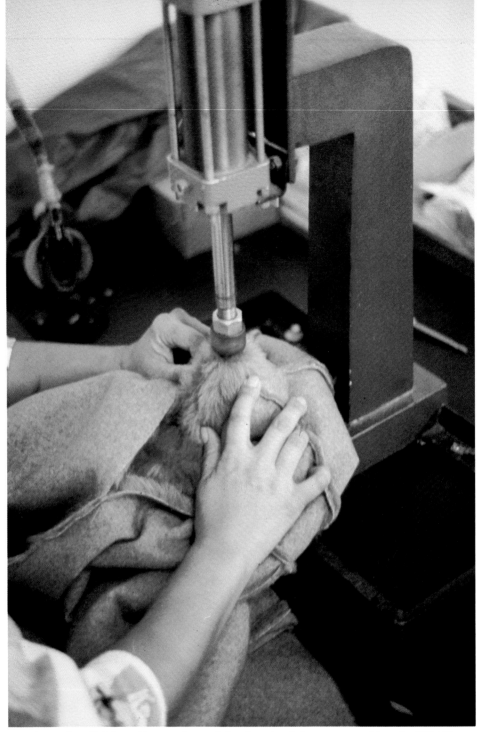

A worker tightens the washer at the back of the eye, making it difficult to be pulled off.

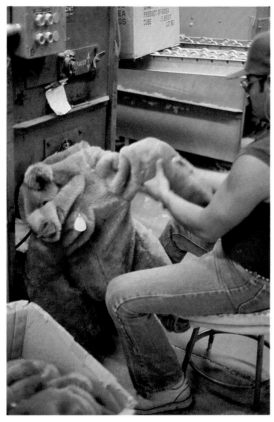
Stuffing the bear

choke on small parts like eyes.

If the bear's nose is to be made of plastic, it will be put on much like the eyes. If the nose is to be made of yarn or leather, it will be stitched on later.

The bear is now ready to be stuffed. It is taken to one of many machines filled with **polyester** stuffing. When a worker presses a foot pedal, the machine blows stuffing into the opening in the bear's back. As the bear's back fills up, the stuffing is pushed to the arms, legs, and head.

It takes a special skill to fill a bear with stuffing. Too much stuffing will make the bear too hard to cuddle comfortably. It will also put extra pressure on the seams and make them wear out sooner. Not enough stuffing will make the plush covering loose and baggy. To get the right amount of stuffing, workers learn how often to push the pedal and how long to hold the pedal down. When the bear

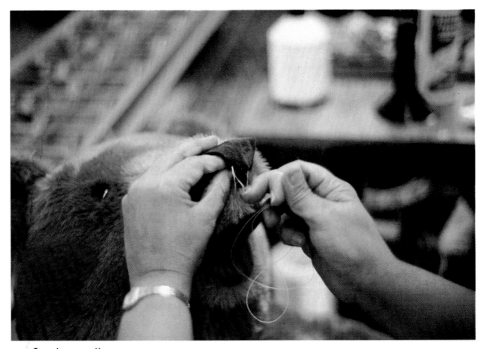

Sewing on the nose

has been stuffed, it is weighed to make sure it has the right amount of stuffing in it.

After the bear has been stuffed, there is more sewing that needs to be done. For one thing, the stuffing hole must be sewn. This is done by hand because the stuffed bear would be hard to sew on a machine and to make sure the stitching will not be noticed. The mouth is now sewn on. So is the nose, if it is to be made of yarn or leather.

The Teddy Bear looks finished, but it isn't. Not quite. Before it's ready to be packaged, it needs to be brushed, picked, and tagged. Brushing helps fluff the plush covering after it has been handled so much. Workers use sharp pointed picks to pull out the hairs of plush that have gotten caught in the seams during sewing. A hang tag—which tells the bear's name, the manufacturer's name, the year, and washing instructions—is added to the bear.

The bear is carefully inspected. Are the eyes even? Are the ears sewn straight? Does the bear look like the prototype? Bears that pass inspection are put into a plastic bag to keep them clean. They are sent through a metal detector to make sure no broken needles have been left in them. Then they are boxed, ready to be shipped. But before ship-

A worker tests the finished bear's eyes to make sure they can't be pulled off easily.

ment, the bears are given one last spot test.

An inspector will choose a few bears. He or she will pull on the small parts of each bear and will measure the amount of tension required to pull the parts off. If a plastic eye or nose can be pulled off with less than 21 pounds of pressure, the bear fails the test and will not be shipped.

Most Teddy Bears pass inspection. They are shipped to warehouses and then to stores all over the world. That's where they wait patiently for you to come and buy them.

- On average, Dakin makes more than six million Teddy Bears each year.

- More than 75 percent of Teddy Bears are made outside the United States.

- Steiff is the largest producer of stuffed toys in the world.

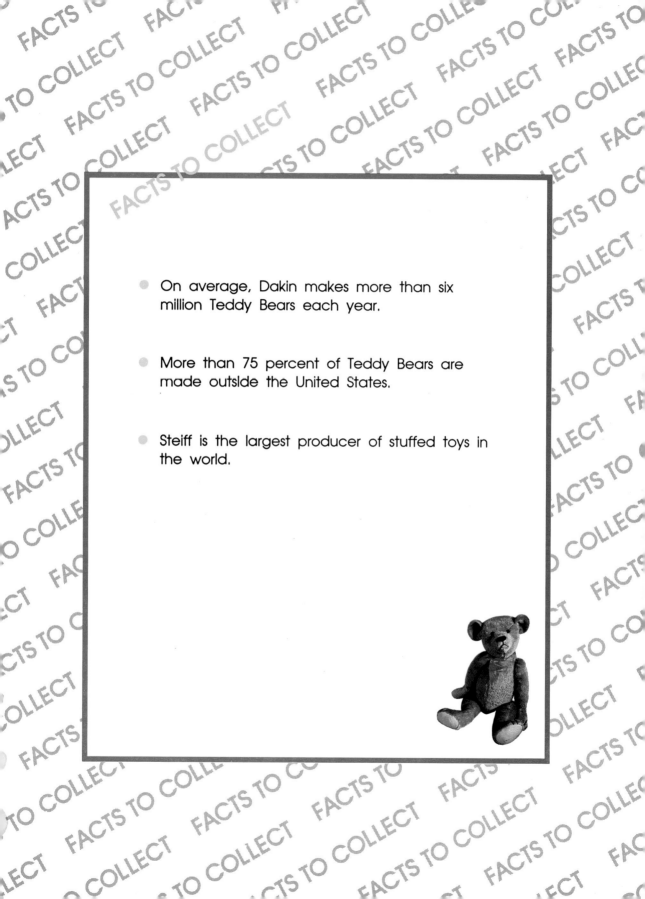

Collecting bears is easy and fun.

CHAPTER 5

Collecting Teddy Bears

Now that you know about Teddy Bears, you might want to collect them. Starting a Teddy Bear collection is easy. First, decide what you want to collect. Do you want to specialize in only one kind of bear, or would you rather collect different kinds? What size bears do you like? What's your favorite color of Teddy Bears? Do you want your Teddy Bears to be jointed? Do you want them to move or talk or make sounds?

After you have decided what kinds of bears you want to collect, figure out how much money you can afford to spend in buying them. This is important because the cost of a Teddy Bear can range from a few dollars to thousands of dollars.

When beginning a Teddy Bear collection, start with bears you already have. Build your collection by getting companions for them. The best way to do this is to buy new, rather than old, bears. New bears usually cost less than old ones. New bears have information with them. It can be found on the tags sewn to the bears and from the boxes some bears are sold in. This information includes the bear's name, who made the bear, and what materials were used in making the bear.

With older bears, information about them is often missing. That makes it harder to know exactly what you are getting and what their true value is.

When you have found a bear you want and can afford, look it over carefully. If it is jointed, move the arms and legs. Does the bear seem sturdy? Check out the seams. Do they seem strong? Does the bear have too much stuffing? If it does, it will put pressure on the seams and make them wear out sooner. Don't forget to look at the bear's face. Does it have an expression you like?

It's easy to find new bears to buy. Toy stores, variety stores, gift stores, and discount stores all sell them. Artist-made bears are sold at Teddy Bear shows, Teddy Bear stores, and through ads in collecting magazines. Buying older bears takes a little more work. Flea markets, garage sales, auctions, antique stores, and Teddy Bear shows are good places to look for them.

Before you go looking for an older bear, learn as much as you can. Read books and magazines, talk to dealers and collectors. Find out the value of

A Teddy Bear display for Christmas

older bears. Learn about the materials used at different times in history so that you have a better chance of knowing what year the bear was made. And remember, never buy a stuffed Teddy Bear the seller claims was made in the 1800s. Why not? The first Teddy Bears weren't made until 1902!

Some people add bears to their collections through advertising. When you know what you're looking for, you can place an ad in a newspaper or collecting magazine.

As your Teddy Bear collection grows, you might want to display your bears. Displaying your collection can be very simple, such as lining up the bears on a bookshelf or on your bed. Try grouping your bears by type, such as Christmas bears, musical bears, handmade bears, and miniature bears.

You can buy special stands to help display your bears. You can also create scenes with your bears. Use your imagination to create a scene of your bears playing, having a party, exploring, or anything else.

It is important to take good care of your Teddy Bear collection. Taking care of your bears means keeping them clean. That is done the same way you keep yourself clean: by bathing. That's right, bathing!

However, unlike humans, not all bears need a bath. If a bear just sits on a shelf and never goes anywhere, it probably doesn't need a bath. In that case, use a small portable vacuum cleaner or hair dryer to remove the dust. A toothbrush will help you groom your bear's fur.

Before you give the dirty bears a bath, give them a light vacuuming, too. Then check their tags. If the manufacturer has provided cleaning instructions, follow them carefully. If not, you will need a soft brush, a bowl, a towel, a washcloth, a fork, and some mild detergent.

Put some warm water and a small amount of detergent in the bowl. With the fork, stir the water until it is sudsy.

Dip the brush into the water, then lightly shake it to get the extra water off. Start at the head of the bear and lightly brush in circles. Put on more suds as you need them and rinse the brush with clean water between dips.

It is important not to put a lot of water on the bear. You want to clean the outer covering; you don't want to soak the stuffing.

When you have gone over the whole bear with the suds and brush, dip the washcloth into clean water and wring it out. Then wipe the suds off the bear by rubbing lightly in circles. When the washcloth gets dirty or soapy, rinse it well and continue.

Pat your bear with a towel. Then put it in a warm spot to dry. Don't put it in direct sunlight because the colors might fade. In a few hours your bear will be dry as well as clean. To speed up drying time, use a hair dryer.

Taking care of your bears also means keeping

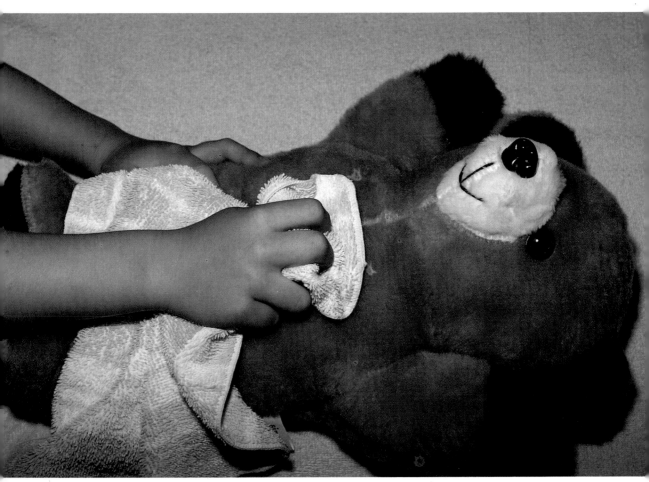

Taking good care of your bears means keeping them clean.

them in good repair. Check them over for rips and missing parts. Sew up the rips, add stuffing if needed, and replace old or lost parts. Stuffing and bear parts can be bought at Teddy Bear stores or craft shops.

If your bear is in really bad shape you might need the help of a Teddy Bear doctor. That's a person who specializes in fixing bears. There are not many Teddy Bear doctors around, so consider yourself lucky if there's one in your area. Check with other collectors or your local crafts store to find out if there's one near you.

By taking care of your bears, you will have them around longer and they will be worth more if you ever want to sell them. But before you do sell your bears, check with a couple of collectors or dealers to see how much they're worth.

Having a Teddy Bear collection is a lot of work. But it is also a lot of fun. You can do many things with your bears. Try dressing them in different outfits. You can find bear clothes in Teddy Bear stores, or you can use clothes that were made for infant dolls. You can also try making the clothes yourself. Remember, Teddy Bears have high waists and short legs, so getting pants that fit right can often be a problem. Shirts, sweaters, and dresses are usually easier to fit. Adding ties, hats, vests, bows, and jewelry are easy ways to dress up your bears.

Have a party for your bears or take them on a picnic. Invite your friends' bears, too. The more the merrier. And don't worry about the food. Teddy Bears don't eat much at all!

Whatever you do, enjoy your Teddy Bears. Play with them, hug them, love them. That's what Teddy Bears were made for.

- Teddy Bears and dolls are the most popular toys to collect.

- There are no "antique" Teddy Bears, since antiques are things that are at least 100 years old.

- More than 40 percent of Dakin's Teddy Bears are sold to adults—for adults.

- Some older bears are valuable. Steiff Teddy Bears that are in excellent condition can sell for more than $100 an inch.

- Some collectors hire buyers called "pickers" to help them find bears. A picker can work for as many as 50 different collectors.

TEDDY BEAR TIME LINE

1800s —Toy bears are popular in many parts of the world.

1897 —Richard Steiff sketches and designs a stuffed bear toy.

1902 —President Teddy Roosevelt hunts for bear in Mississippi; Clifford Berryman creates the famous "hunting" cartoon; Rose and Morris Michtom produce a stuffed bear and call it "Teddy's Bear"; the Margarete Steiff Company produces its first stuffed bear.

1906 —Clothes and other accessories are made for Teddy Bears.

1909 —Teddy Bears are made in England.

1920 —New materials are used in making Teddy Bears; Christopher Robin Milne receives a Teddy Bear that becomes the basis for his father's famous Winnie-the-Pooh stories.

1925 —The Gebrüder Sussenguth Company makes Peter, a realistic bear with sharp teeth and a fierce growl.

1930s —People become concerned about toy safety;

toy makers work with the National Safety Council.

1969 —James T. Ownby forms Good Bears of the World (GBW) to give bears to people who need special friends.

1970s —Teddy bear collecting becomes popular; more handcrafted bears are made.

1973 —The Consumer Product Safety Commission (CPSC) is formed to help enforce toy safety rules.

1979 —Barbara Isenberg designs Albert the Running Bear, the first bear in the North American Bear Company line.

1983 —Kenner produces the Care Bears, the bears with a message.

1984 —Carolyn and Lawrence Shaffer create Sir Koff-A-Lot to help heart surgery patients.

1985 —Teddy Ruxpin, the first bear made using computer technology, is sold by Worlds of Wonder.

1989 —Rosemary and Paul Volpp buy a 1926 Steiff bear for $86,350; Yankee Doodle Teddy, the world's largest bear, is constructed by Keystone Traders Ltd.

1990 —Frannie's Teddy Bear Museum opens in Naples, Florida.

FOR MORE INFORMATION

For more information about toys, write to:

Communications Dept.
Toy Manufacturers of America
200 Fifth Avenue
New York, NY 10010
(toy fact booklet, "Betcha Didn't Know")

For more information about careers in toy making, write to:

Judy Ellis, Chairperson
Toy Design Department
Fashion Institute of Technology
Seventh Avenue and 27th Street
New York, NY 10001

For more information about Teddy Bears and particular brands, write to:

Applause, Inc.
6101 Variel Avenue
P.O. Box 4183
Woodland Hills, CA 91365

Enesco Corp.
1 Enesco Plaza
Elk Grove Village, IL 60007
(bear-related products)

The Bear Care Co.
279 S. Beverly Dr., Suite 957-R
Beverly Hills, CA 90212
(bear cleaning products)

Gund, Inc.
P.O. Box H
Edison, NJ 08818
North American Bear Co.

Muffin Enterprises
429 S. 18th Street
Camp Hill, PA 17011
(Sir Koff-A-Lot)

North American Bear Co.
Public Relations Dept.
401 N. Wabash, Suite 500
Chicago, IL 60611

Toy Faire
39300 Paseo Padre Parkway
Fremont, CA 94538
(Teddy Ruxpin)

For more information about Teddy Bear magazines and clubs, write to:

Bear Tracks
Box 13097
Toledo, OH 43613

Muffy Vanderbear Fan Club
c/o North American Bear Co.
401 N. Wabash, Suite 500
Chicago, IL 60611

Teddy Bear and Friends
Hobby House Press, Inc.
900 Frederick Street
Cumberland, MD 21502

Teddy Bear Review
P.O. Box 1239
Hanover, PA 17331

The Teddy Tribune
254 W. Sidney
St. Paul, MN 55107

Places to visit:

Carrousel
505 W. Broad St.
Chesaning, MI 48616

Frannie's Teddy
Bear Museum
2511 Pine Ridge Road
Naples, FL 33942

Museum of
American History
Smithsonian Institution
Washington, DC 20560
(early Michtom bear)

Strong Museum
One Manhattan Square
Rochester, NY 14607

GLOSSARY

arctophilist (ark-toe-FY-list)—a person who collects Teddy Bears

die—a sharp metal device used to cut out pieces of plush

kapok (KAY-pock)—silky fibers that cover the seeds of the kapok tree; used as a Teddy Bear stuffing

mohair (MO-hair)—the hair of Angora goats; used as a covering for Teddy Bears

plush—the soft, furlike fabric used as a covering for most stuffed toys; the term used by the toy industry for all stuffed toys

polyester (POL-ee-es-ter)—an artificial fiber used in stuffing Teddy Bears

prototype (PRO-tuh-type)—the first model on which a product is patterned

INDEX

ABOUT THE AUTHOR

A fourth-grade teacher and free-lance writer, Robert Young is fascinated by kids and the things they collect. In addition to the books in the Collectibles series, Mr. Young has written about a wide range of subjects. *The Chewing Gum Book* and *Sneakers: The Shoes We Choose!* are two of his titles recently published under the Dillon Press imprint. Mr. Young lives with his family in Eugene, Oregon, and enjoys visiting schools and talking to teachers and students about writing.